TALENT MUKARO
Reinforcement onto God's promises
Unleashing new transitions

Table of Contents

Preface

This book was written by a genuine and credible young man well-groomed in a Christian society. He believes and always confess that he is not an ordinary Christian but rather an extra-ordinary Christian - believer. He was born and raised in Masvingo province – the province from which the name - Zimbabwe was picked. He is a life coach by calling, unique online motivational speaker and inspirational writer by passion. Talent is highly eager in seeing people of all ages and religions coming to the same platform of living their lives at their optimum and full potentials. He is keen and aspiring to create a vibrant leadership in Zimbabwe as well as Africa.

Currently, he is undertaking his first bachelor of technology(Hons.) in Electronic Engineering with the Harare Institute of Technology. When this book was written, his aim was to inform and later see all people enjoying the promises of God, God promised us and our forefathers many years back. He also believes that for something to be firm and to last long there has to be some reinforcement. Likewise, in this context, for the promises of God to be firm and last long in someone's life, there is a need of a reinforcement. As a result, he then wrote this book for you and him too, take care and enjoy this gift. May the good Lord richly bless you in all your life endeavours, amen.

Introduction

Promises have been a rhythm from the onset of the world. God as the creator, usually used to utter promises whenever His creation was pleasing to him. He is recorded giving the first promise to Adam in the garden of Eden and this was a promise of having dominion over everything. Today, He is still giving out His promises to the world through the influence of the Holy Ghost. Above all promises, the most of all and prominent promise of God I believe its fulfilment is that of giving the whole world only His one begotten son to die for us on the cross for the remission of our sins. So as a writer, I found grace in the Lord to write this book titled, **"Reinforcement onto God's promises"** and sub-titled, *"Unleashing New Transitions".*

This book is trying to equip you and as well to challenge your spirit not to live as a Christian only, for that has been highly polluted by many but rather live as a believer in Christ. Most Christians per say not all, they live like Christ but believers believe in Christ, so in other terms, they live in Christ. So reinforcement onto God's promises is just showcasing what one has to do in order to have manifestation of those promises of God the life being lived. Under God's guidance and inspiration, I wrote this book comprising of the following chapters namely:

- Promise Definition

- Promise Qualifications
- Promise Identification
- Promise Highway
- Promise Acquisition
- Promise Conduction.

The above topics are just giving out some insight on reinforcement onto God's promises for an individual or even for a group of people but with one purpose for instance as a family or a church. May God richly bless you as you will be going through this book, I believe it will be a blessing to your body, spirit and soul. May all your promises from God come into existence in the name of Jesus Christ, as you will be reading through this book and meditating. Enjoy your sail my brethren, more grace and life to you.

Chapter 1: *Promise Definition*

Objectives:

- To lay a solid foundation on what really a promise of God is and what is the concept behind.
- To fish out the relevance of a promise of God in our lives (when it is supposed to be grabbed).
- To understand the basic fundamentals of getting the promises of God.
- To unravel the real mysteries in having the real promises of God.

A Promise – Is a verbal utterance God uttered through His prophets with a great commitment long back ago to our fathers and to our forefathers in faith. In other words, a promise is a futuristic verbal commitment that God gave to us. Some philosophical views are that a promise can be an expectation basing on the prophecies of God to His people. Yes, it might be true as they say that a promise of God is a prophecy of God, but, I believe those two words are different channels to encounter God through. A prophecy is a gift of the Holy Spirit that its purpose is to edify the church while a promise is an assurance from God concerning His previous committed utterances. When God gives out His prophecies, He normally chooses the side He wants to touch and go deeper into. A prophecy can either be good or bad to the receiver but a promise is definitely for the good. This means that God's promises are all to the good of God and His people as well – both parties gain.

When God reveal His prophecies there are probabilities that God will change His mind according to my character/your own character transition. For instance, God's prophecy through His prophet, Prophet Isaiah concerning the numbered days of King Hezekiah. When King Hezekiah heard that, he turned to the wall and prayed to God. He prayed and cried before the Lord. Then, the Lord changed His mind for He had seen the sincerity which the King had shown. Then, for the promises of God, God at times just speaks out and has already spoken them out to His children because of the reason that He created them in His own image having good and great plans for each and every person on earth. My dear brethren, your character transitions may not block the promises of God to manifest in your life but they just delay the manifestations of the promises of God in your life.

Coming to the Bible, the Holy Word of God, Jesus Christ Himself in His fullness (John 1:1) in form of letters and words, which were once thoughts of God and then God expressed it in words. Those words were demonstrated through the power of the Holy Ghost. And as a result the Word was made flesh and dwelt amongst us (John 1:14). In the Word we encounter many promises to the world from God. Many enjoyed that, some are still enjoying and will be going to enjoy these promises of God I am talking about forevermore. God gave the first promise to Adam, the man whom God give all His dominion in the human kind form, God said that be fruitful and multiply. The fruitfulness and multiplication God spoke of was not this one we saw today, but it was supposed to be a spiritual one that Adam was supposed to speak whatsoever he was desiring to see on earth and materialisation was to take place.

Look, when God created the heavens and the earth (Genesis 1:1), He then went on to say that let there be light and light materialise thus it came into existence and this brought shape to the formless earth. My dear, if you want shape in your life speak a word upon your life to gain shape again. Whatsoever shape you desire, God will back you up with the materialisation of your words if you really believe Him and you are sincere. What is light, light is Jesus Christ, Oh what an honour! Scientifically light is a dimension that help us to see, light gives shape to all the things and this philosophy is just a borrowed phenomenon from the Word of God.

The another promise of God was given to Abraham, that I will make your descendants great and you will be numerous like the stars of the sky. Abraham then grew from a childhood into a teenager, from a teenager into a young adult and then left a young adult into the middle age holding to that promise of God. I hope he got married at an early age and sailed in his faith and hope in God, then when he was about 75 years, God came to give him a prophecy of the promises of God, He promised him before the foundations of the world. Allow me to say this, I do believe that it was in Sarah the issue of accepting the barrenness as her lifestyle package from her tender ages.

My brethren, never accept some systems the devil uses to delay your promises from God to manifest in your life. Some systems you apply for them personally using your own free will choices. In other terms, I believe your unbelief in God is the one that will hinder you and delay you from getting your promises from God. See, when the angel of God said that Sarah was going to have a child we saw that she was a gossiper, how did she laughed on the story of the four outside the tent whilst she was in the tent preparing a meal. That on its own shows out that she was someone who was eager to hear even such which were not of her accord and want as well to talk too much. You see, her unbelief was proven.

Look here, she insisted Abraham to have a child with her maidservant, Haggai for she was hopeless of having a child of her own womb for the years had gone out. My brother, my sister be careful the time the devil starts to show up to you giving you some ideas thus the same time God is rising up from His sitting on His throne to rescue you. The time Satan get in contact with what God is about to do for you, he is run ahead before God came in to deceive you with a substitute similar in appearance to the one of God but it won't last long for it is a fake provision.

But when the angel of God had spoken out this message from God, she then changed her heart and uttered that she hasn't laughed. Oh Lord! What a white lie! but to me I can say this changed her. Look a wife of the Father of great faith lying to an angel of the Lord. But after a lie, the angel knew that she will run away from her unbelief. After that had happened, signs and wonders started to manifest on the old granny and she conceived. For Abraham, he had lived a promised life 75 years when his life started to transform into a promise-filled and prophecy-filled life.

See how embarrassing it is to see promises and prophecies not coming to the fulfilment. After receiving the prophecy of having many descendants, I thought and hope, him and his spouse thought at first they were to woke up tomorrow conceived and have twins but it stretched, decades and decades. Promises of God will always stand and can't be broken or altered by any man. But what man can do to God's will is to delay, as God will be waiting for the man purification. Man can also delay due to the state of minds and attitudes since no scripture can be broken, but the scripture can be a bigger one or a smaller one as far as its influence in someone's life. Then, here due to Sarah's unbelief Abraham sinned in having an affectionate with Haggai and because of that God delayed the coming of Isaac and this took decades to have a fulfilment.

I don't care what is your unbelief; how big it is, to what extent it is affecting your life, how long have you imprisoned with it, but what I am sure and certain of is that if you cast it out of your mind thus your way of life and believe in Jesus Christ as the way maker of each and every way of life and promise keeper of each and every promise He promised to our forefathers and to our fathers, He will show you that it was your unbelief that was hindering you from getting your promises manifestation. As a sum up, a promise of God is fit for those that have recognised the Word of God and have took a step in the Word of God.

My dear, my advice to you is be rooted in the Word of God thus be in the Word in words and in actions. Brethren, be advised to live according to the Word of God, leave a compromised lifestyle and go for a separated lifestyle. Where a compromised lifestyle is, there is a copying activation hence competition. O Lord, promises are not there for competition, but rather they are there for the completion of ourselves in the Lord to meet the right stature of a perfect man. No promise of God will manifest in your life if you are still holding on to your mind-set that is competitive in Christ, so my advice is have a completion mind-set in Christ.

Prayer:

O Lord, my God, God of Abraham (The great father of real faith), Isaac (The son of promise of God) and Jacob (The father of the 12 tribes of Israel); I come to you at this hour, asking for forgiveness and reconciliation, for I know that I have been astray out of your promises way. Oh my God may you kindly help me to understand these true facts about your promises and those many facts that are to come to enhance my knowledge of what a promise is. I pray for you my sister, my brother, may your history or background lose you today in the name of Jesus Christ of Nazareth. May they both allow you to have an encounter with God as He will be calling you as a deliverer of your family. May God's grace locate you to rub off your history from Saul to Paul. And may Saul to Paul anointing fall upon you today in Jesus Christ's blessed and great name above all names. You were born to be a prophet to many nations, you were groomed to be priests and kings here on earth and you are destined for great exploits.

Today through this script, O Lord! I am being moulded to become one of those who will prophesy in these end times we are in. I shall be known all over the world, for I am one of a peculiar generation. My dear Father in heaven, I believe that I am not of this world, since the one who is in me is greater than the one who is in the world. I am born of spirit, full of spirit and I live in spirit, for I am of spirit. O Lord, many promises you have promised us but the truth is that all your promises are for those only who are aligned to your Word somewhere, somehow. Lord may you restore the zeal for you that has been in me that I may learn more about your and have a personal encounter with you in Jesus' name. Oh my Father, help me to be truly aligned to your Word in Jesus Christ's blessed name I pray and know that I am certain that it is done in favour of me. Amen.

Declarations:

I declare and I decree in Jesus Christ's name that;

- No more delays in all the promises of God concerning my life.
- I am leaving a compromised lifestyle and transitioning into a separated lifestyle.

- No more conflicts in my belief because of my able Jesus Christ and I am highly elevated in my faith and knowledge in the Lord.
- All promises that have been delayed before are now in an acceleration mode to their manifestation in my life.
- My life will never be the same again for the truth is setting me free and I shall not lack anything for all my needs are in God's promises.
- All physical and spiritual promises God gave to Israel are mine and I am content to enjoy them.
- I am not hesitant to act upon each and every promise of God He promised to us through His Word.
- My future is brighter than my past and present, I will be announced when other will be ashamed.
- My tomorrow is glorious than my yesterday and my today, I will be fruitful in all my life endeavours.
- I will surely possess the gates of my enemies, it might not be today but definitely I will do it soon.
- I will witness all the promises of God in my life and enjoy all of them to the fullness.
- I am now inspired to aspire to be a blessing to the whole world and I am living to bless people, world at large and not to be blessed by the world.

- I got the revelation that the all promises of God are mine and I am highly elevated in Christ and for Christ.
- No more limitations in the name of Jesus Christ and I am destined for greater exploits to be explored.
- Now am highly enlightened to be at a point of knowing what to do to get my promise manifestation. No more delays in all the promises of God concerning my life.
- I am leaving a compromised lifestyle and transitioning into a separated lifestyle, Amen.

Chapter 2: Promise Qualifications

Objectives:

- To know terms and conditions for you to acquire the promises of God.
- To understand what does it take for you to see your promise from God.
- To accept the idea of patience in waiting for the fulfilment of God's promises.

From chapter one, we saw that a promise is the assurance from God, thus a sealed expectation in the Lord. This is the one that gives me the certainty that one day somewhere, somehow I am going to receive from the Lord. The promises we are talking of are utterances from God the Almighty one who is holy in all and His works are great and marvellous (Revelations 19:1ff). Since the one who promised these promises is holy, I believe somewhere, somehow He love those who are holy to receive His promises in time.

I hope and I believe that all promises of God are fulfilled to the person rather to a believer that is in line with the Word of God. Dear brethren, what is it that takes for me or you to have a promised of God? A promise to my own understanding comes in existence due to the fact that someone has satisfied his master somewhere, somehow. A promise is given as a token of appreciation in advance thus just a round of applause to the believer.

Our fathers did wonders before God and God was to promise them wonders in form of His promises to them and to us as well, since God's blessings are inheritable to them that are good to Him and believe in Him. Being a child of God only being just has got a divine providence to be promised by our Father in heaven for He can't let us live us alone without our comforter, Holy Spirit so He was to promise the coming of the Holy Spirit to comfort us, amen. Going deeper now, what are the requirements for the promises to be dedicated to you (I am certain it is just due to your alignment in the Word of God).

Coming to the pivot of our lives, the Word of God, Jesus Christ Himself we see, Hannah a daughter of God – a prayer warrior and a reveller as well. It is written and said that she was barren and she was in a polygamous courtship and her counterpart was mocking her in the chapter one of 1 Samuel to the extent of crying due to emotions. The Bible as well alluded that this was her obstacle for she would went to Shiloh each and every year and pray for her disgrace to be wiped off. Having no child sometimes is better than having children you will not be able to control or cater for, for the

Bible at one point shows out that blessed are those that did not bear a child.

My brethren sometimes what you take a disgrace in your physical eyes it is rather a blessing in disguise. Hannah, I think and believe that she saw a promise of being fruitful and multiply as it was promised to our father of faith – Abraham and at first she didn't know what was required for the promise to materialise. She would go to Shiloh, pray and come back with no evidence of God's promise manifestation in her life. She prayed for Samuel, as the Lord had promised fruitfulness and multiplication, and as His Word figures out that sons are an inheritance from the Lord.

Here, we are saw Hannah and the promise was there to have an inheritance from her Lord, thus a son Samuel, but God's sovereignty intervened and God cause a delay for Hannah not to use all strategies and approaches she was applying, thus to remove a competitive mind-set. Where do we find this competitive mind-set? In a polygamous family, there is competition. Once competition comes into your day to day operations, the devil will grab that chance to become the pivot of that lifestyle since we know Jesus Christ requires us to have a completion mind-set since in Him we are one and complete.

Hannah and Peninah, I do believe that they were in a competition in child bearing when Peninah got her sons – I don't know under what measure and how, but what I know is that she was given the inheritance from the Lord by the Lord and for Hannah it was seeming like nothing was in her package from the Lord, but in the silence God was moulding a best prophet to help His people and coming through Hannah. Brother, sister when God is delaying testimonies in our lives as a strategy to avoid stress and depression, your testimony is in the oven in the kitchen and you are in the lounge and the door of the kitchen seems as if it is closed.

God is giving you time my dear to clean the dining room and decorate it according to the food that is being prepared by God Himself for you. If the food is traditional, then put those fancy traditional decorations and if it is this modern food we are seeing being prepared then the choice is yours on the decorations. Let us all apply that same concept in our spiritual lifestyle. When you have encountered that your promises from God (in His Word) are taking time, those are delaying in your life, just view it this way that God is cooking a pleasant testimony for you. What is needed of you? My dear, since testimony is coming, your duty is to cleanse yourself, repent from your ways, confess your sins, believe in God, and surrender all to Jesus Christ.

Oh my! What did Hannah do? she was having a bad mind-set by the revelation of God and she would come to Shiloh with Peninah and the whole family, then one day, God revealed something to her that for a promise to manifest there was to be a transformation of her mind and cease to go back home with the Peninahs. She then told the family and Peninah go ahead, that she was to catch up with them on the way back soon. Sometimes, you need to separate yourself from many people and cling to God only. But what you need first is the revelation of Jesus Christ for the activation of God's promises in your life.

In the Christian lifetime, what matters most is not praying but, rather the motive behind that prayer. Have this in my that it is not about just praying to God but it has to be who is praying and why is s/he praying. Some prayers I think and believe that they are like noise in God's ears, since God looks at the sincerity and motive of the prayer and of the one praying not the vocabulary or quantity of words. Because of this, thus why you hear God saying that don't heap many words in prayer but just say this and that (Read Matthew 6).

I am certain and sure that God most of the times, He takes His in trying to figure out who is praying, why s/he is praying that prayer and not was is in the prayer. Hannah prayed for the promise of a son to manifest in her life to remove her disgrace from the eyes of the colleagues but due that mind-set i.e. competition based, God delayed the manifestation of this promise, but He rather highly upgraded the quality her testimony. Then, God gave her a revelation of talking to the priest Eli. This came to the extent, that she fished out that the son was going to be God's son and will be going to live in God's house. Eish, look what a motive!

God's promises mainly are given out to blessers and blessings, those that have been desiring and are desiring to be blessings in people's lives. In the Word of God, many characters saw God's blessings manifesting in their lives due to the fact that they first desired to be blessings and then God established their desires and now they are blessers in the name of Jesus Christ of Nazareth, amen. Here, there is a simple instruction I propose for you, be a blesser of others if you want and wills to receive God's promises. Abraham was a blesser, Isaac was a blesser, Jacob was a blesser, Rebekah was a blesser as well, Hannah became a blesser as well, Daniel was a blesser, Peter and Paul they were all blessers.

Aspire to be a blesser and not to be blessed by others. Desire to help yourself and not to be helped by others, for thus the only way to run away from being beggars. God usually spent most of His time on the people that are desiring to be blessers to the world. When Hannah chose to be a blesser in the church of God, God loosened the delay belts and the promise fell down into her life. My sister, my brother let this be your aspiration that you may be a blessing and a blesser in a good proper way for you to be a real partaker of God's promises. I assure you promise after promise fulfilment will be your portion since is loosening the delay belt that has been fastened in your life. I don't care how big/small it might be, but what I know God will surely back you up if you are really sincere and you really mean it.

Prayer:

Ooh My Father, the Father of the fatherless, the real husband to the widows in all their lives endeavours. I come to you at this juncture of my life, O Lord! May you fulfil all my pleadings for many great aspirations. I pray for myself, my family, may our history or background lose us today in the name of Jesus Christ of Nazareth. May they both allow us to have an encounter with you God as you will be calling me as a deliverer of our family. May God's grace locate me to rub off my history from Saul to Paul. And may Saul to Paul anointing fall upon me today in Jesus Christ's blessed and great name above all names. I was born to be a prophet to many nations, I was groomed to be a priest and a king here on earth and I am destined for great exploits. Today through this script, O Lord! I am being moulded to become one of those who will prophesy in these end times we are in.

I shall be known all over the world, for I am one of a peculiar generation. My dear Father in heaven, I believe that I am not of this world, since the one who is in me is greater than the one who is in the world. I am born of spirit, full of spirit and I live in spirit, for I am of spirit. O Lord, many promises you have promised us but the truth is that all your promises are for those only who are aligned to your Word somewhere, somehow. Lord may you restore the zeal for you that has been in me that I may learn more about your and have a personal encounter with you in Jesus' name. My good Lord and the only shepherd I know may you highly bless and protect me, may all doors in my life be opened in the name of Jesus Christ of Nazareth. Amen.

Declarations:

I declare and I decree in the name of Jesus Christ of Nazareth that:

- I am now inspired to aspire to be a blessing to the whole world and I am living to bless people, world at large and not to be blessed by the world.
- I got the revelation that the all promises of God are mine and I am highly elevated in Christ and for Christ.
- No more limitations in the name of Jesus Christ and I am destined for greater exploits to be explored.

- Now am highly enlightened to be at a point of knowing what to do to get my promise manifestation. No more delays in all the promises of God concerning my life.
- I am leaving a compromised lifestyle and transitioning into a separated lifestyle.
- No more conflicts in my belief because of my able Jesus Christ and I am highly elevated in my faith and knowledge in the Lord.
- All promises that have been delayed before are now in an acceleration mode to their manifestation in my life.
- My life will never be the same again for the truth is setting me free and I shall not lack anything for all my needs are in God's promises.
- All physical and spiritual promises God gave to Israel are mine and I am content to enjoy them and I am not hesitant to act upon each and every promise of God He promised to us through His Word.
- My future is brighter than my past and present, I will be announced when other will be ashamed.
- My tomorrow is glorious than my yesterday and my today, I will be fruitful in all my life endeavours.

- I will surely possess the gates of my enemies, it might not be today but definitely I will do it soon and I will witness and enjoy all the promises of God to the fullness.
- My mentality has shifted to a higher positive realm, and I am no longer looking for minor things but I am after better things in the Lord.
- The Lord has granted me all promises He promised to me and my forefathers.
- My attitude, hope and faith have changed, for the Lord has inspired me to be a better believer.
- Many will come to congratulates me on this great boom, for these promises of God are a great boom, Amen.

Chapter 3: Promise Identification

Objectives:

- To understand how one can identify the promise in its original identity.
- To get a revelation if the promise is in its due season to manifest in our lives.
- To get into the way the promise identified is demanding us to walk in.
- To identify the value of having the identity of the promise of God.

Well, I am highly convinced that today you are going to encounter a promise of God in a certain arena of your life, by starting with identification, analysis and then decision making on embarking the promise of God. There are promises that God gave to the physical Israel but, not to the spiritual Israel. Physical Israel was to be in bondage for more than 400years and not the spiritual Israel. Someone might say, what are these two - the physical Israel and the spiritual Israel? What are their differences then? Physical Israel is that generation of the people who are Israel by birth, these are possessors of the Canaan fertile lands. Then, the spiritual Israel I am alluding to is that Israel in which you and me are in today (thus the generation of the gentiles).

The generation that have believed in the Word of God without any physical circumcision evidence. What is evident in their lives is the spiritual circumcision of our hearts.

Going back to the essence of the story, once you have identified the promises you have to look at your time and see what time is it? Check the time, the season and the available opportunity to grab your promise. For a promise of God to be manifested rightly in your life you have to identify the time, season and opportunity, if all the three are in agreement then take an effort to be ready to do exploits. But, before you do exploits, first you have to know who you are. Thus identify your identity and the kind of a promise you are in line with and keen to see its manifestation in your life. You can't expect a promise of rain to fall upon you when you are in the winter season, this is physical though. Getting spiritual now, you can't expect to receive manna when you are still before the Red Sea, enter the wilderness and then have an encounter with God. You can't receive manna and enjoy it before an encounter with God. You need God first, then enjoy the Godly provided manna.

But here, know this, that these miracles that are there now, they are there for a season and are to mark your existence in the wilderness. You can't continue to have manna, when you will be a step away from Jordan river. What am I saying, thus what I define, *"promise identification"?* Taking a glimpse in the Word of God, here we look Shamgar, just an Israelite by birth, not a soldier or a warrior. He looked at the time and he saw his time in a due season full of a Godly provided opportunity. He killed 600 philistines for the first time in the history of Israel. It was like never before, it was an unusual encounter with the philistines. Since, for many years these philistines have developed a habit of raiding Israel in the time just before harvest. Philistine had abandoned her lands, and Israel had taken them for her agriculture produce.

So this time around, the Philistine army prepared to raid Israel as usual and they took their way to Israel. When the Israel army saw them approaching, they trembled and already they were admitting to submit and surrender to the Philistines, thus letting these strangers enjoy their harvests year after year. Look here, the Prophet of God, Reverend William Marrion Branham in the Message titled, ***"Convinced, then concerned",*** He clearly fished out how Shamgar identified the promise of God and examined the scenario. After the examination, he saw where he was; the time it was, season he was in and opportunity in the promise of God that had been placed before him.

Shamgar then, knew that it was the right time, right season, right opportunity, in the right anointing through the right inspiration that the promise of God was in need of activation thus, from a written record to an action record. He saw that there was a hanging promise of God in line with the right dealing with the enemies of Israel without consideration of being spiritual or physical Israel. Shamgar came to a point that he realised God has already promised Israel to possess the gates of their enemies thus in this context to confront the battles and conquer massively each and every enemy.

The Prophet went on to say that, he (Shamgar) had identified the promise, was determined and was a vision to conquer the philistines mightily. The he told his wife what he was envisioning, his mission and the strategies to accomplish it. By an ox-goad, he smote 600 mighty philistine army soldiers and the other 300 giants retreated, thus in all he defeated the Philistines. Remember, Philistine is historically the homeland of Goliath that great man who at one point in time was a threat to Israel. But here Shamgar of no bigger stature did it through the grace of God. When the grace of God locates you, your stature is of no accordance, for grace of God qualifies the unqualified but called. Your mockers will be your workers when the promises of God commence to manifest in your life.

Before he left to meet the Philistines head on, the Prophet of God said that maybe Shamgar's wife might have said that darling don't go you will die and I will a widow and none of the people in the city will cater for us since we are inferior. She might have alluded that she was not yet prepared to be a widow and to see her sons and daughters being called orphans just because of a death threat willing their Father had willingly decided to take. His siblings might have cried and said that dad please don't go. But, however because of the inspiration God had installed in him, he gave them a deaf ear and said that they were going to have a victorious party when he comes back. He assigned them to start preparing for a banquet they were to enjoy on his return from the battlefield.

There are times in life when we have to cease fasting, praying and crying to God but rejoice in the Lord, take an action and make decision with the back-up of God through the right inspiration. Decision is the uttermost demarcation of someone's fall/rise while prayers and fasting are spices for a greater taste of the fall/rise. Shamgar might have been fasting and praying for years concerning the Philistines attacks whenever they were approaching harvest time, yet there was seeming no answer. Yes, there was no answer for that, but there was a promise from God. God had already answered them, but due to the fact that the answer was in God's promises they did not catch the mystery for they were still asking for an already provided package.

People of today are asking for already provided thing, but hidden secretly in the promises of God. Stop crying my dear brethren, it's no longer a season of crying, but it is it's a season to have faith in the Lord, take an action and see your tears being wiped away. When God said that Israel was to possess the gates of their enemies, all was granted to them right there but what is left for us is to believe, take our own right positions and decide on the next step either accelerate it/take it/delay it. By the hand of one man, the whole nation of Israel was delivered from the hand of their enemy. They possessed the gates of their enemies by the use of an ox-goad, thus 1000 philistines were defeated.

My brother, my sister when the promises of God were unleashed to our grand forefathers in faith it seemed very complicated and impossible for them to manifest in the physical life but they believed them. They believed and lived in these promises. For instance, Abraham believed the promise of fruitfulness and multiplication and as a result, he lived the promise in a full measure. Shamgar believed the promise of possessing the enemies' gates and as a result, he lived in the full potential of the promise manifestation. Same in your life my brethren, have a belief in the Lord for any promise of God you desire to see being manifested in your life and then live it to your full potential. An ox-goad smote 600 giants, what a miracle! If you just believe in the promise of

God, it doesn't matter how small or big your situation is. God is greater than anything you might imagine and dream of. "What is it that you have Moses?", God asked Moses as Israel had faced Red Sea.

The same principles of God that were applied to Israel are the ones still that will be applied in each and every situation in your life. Our God is a master strategist; He has got His own principles of doing things for His creatures. Whenever you identify the promise of God, act upon it whether difficulties/challenges arose or not. I assure you that you will live it to your full potential. Always be ready and expectant. One day, God will ask you my son, my daughter, *"what is it that you have in your hand?"* Today am saying this to you my dear, *"what do you have in your hand"?* Your answer has to come this way, "I have you my Lord Jesus Christ (Word of God) in my hand, in my heart, in my mind, in my soul and in my strength". He will manifest Himself in your life, for your good in the reinforcement of His promises in your entire life.

Prayer:

Dear God, O what a wonderful experience I had with you today through this Word. O Lord, my father, my healer, my provider, I pray now help me to identify my promises from you. Help me O Lord to act upon them all Lord for you have place in my heart that only a decision is the uttermost demarcation for one's fate or rise. O Lord, we may have plans but you always come with a final decision. O Lord my God, father to the fatherless and husband to the widows. I pray thee, O Lord may give us patience and strength to persevere. We know when things got tough for us, thus the ample given time for us to go higher in spirit and cause commotion in the kingdom of the devil.

Today through this script, O Lord! I am being moulded to become one of those who will prophesy in these end times we are in. I shall be known all over the world, for I am one of a peculiar generation. My dear Father in heaven, I believe that I am not of this world, since the one who is in me is greater than the one who is in the world. I am born of spirit, full of spirit and I live in spirit, for I am of spirit. O Lord, many promises you have promised us but the truth is that all your promises are for those only who are aligned to your Word somewhere, somehow. O Lord, may you restore the zeal for you that has been in me. Help me that I may learn more about you and have a personal encounter with you in Jesus' name. Help me, O Lord to be like Shamgar, help me Lord to be a Shamgar of our family, society, nation in the great name of Jesus Christ of Nazareth, I pray. Amen.

Declarations:

I declare and I decree in the name of Jesus Christ of Nazareth that:

- All promises God gave to physical Israel are mine.
- I won't hesitate to act upon all the promises God gave me and I will be fruitful and multiply in the promises of God.
- My future is greater than my present, and my tomorrow is more glorious than my today.
- I will possess the gates of my enemies (lock the devil and keep his gate keys) and I will behave in the right way In line with my destiny promises.
- I will go to many nations, many nations will know my name and my impact and I will be prosperous through Christ who strengths me always in the name of Jesus Christ.
- No more delays in all the promises of God concerning my life and I am leaving a compromised lifestyle and transitioning into a separated lifestyle.
- No more conflicts in my belief because of my able Jesus Christ and I am highly elevated in my faith and knowledge in the Lord.

- All promises that have been delayed before are now in an acceleration mode to their manifestation in my life.
- My life will never be the same again for the truth is setting me free and I shall not lack anything for all my needs are in God's promises.
- All physical and spiritual promises God gave to Israel are mine and I am content to enjoy them and I am not hesitant to act upon each and every promise of God He promised to us through His Word.
- My future is brighter than my past and present, I will be announced when other will be ashamed.
- My tomorrow is glorious than my yesterday and my today, I will be fruitful in all my life endeavours.
- I will surely possess the gates of my enemies, it might not be today but definitely I will do it soon and I will witness all the promises of God in my life, Amen.

Chapter 4: Promise Highway

Objectives:

- To know the value of believing God promises with sincerity.
- To understand the essence of waiting upon the Lord concerning His promises.
- To get the revelation of where the promise is and how to get there.

Am glad that this chapter will bless you, since it is all about the highway to the promise. What is this way? Remember, our Lord Jesus Christ said that He is the way, the truth and the life, so here what is this way now to the promise? A way is a channel, a tunnel, a line, an entrance that can give you access to a certain needy you are eager to have. Here, it is a way to your promise. Brethren, the only possible way to your promise is Jesus Christ. Remember He said, "I am the way, the truth and the life", since no one can go to heaven without going through Christ. Apostle Paul said that it is a gain to die in Christ since Christ is the way to heaven, amen. For every promise there is a way, if you want life to manifest in your life in abundance, there is Jesus Christ as the way to life.

Give Jesus Christ your life as a tithe and see the transition of long life in your life. He will open the flood gates of heaven full of life for you. If you want the truth, there is a way to truth, there look there is Jesus Christ as the way to the truth and truth as well. So here, brethren if you want a promise from God, there is a proper and definite way to the promise and that way is the Word of God, thus the living Jesus Christ and that promise is Jesus Christ as well. The Word of God is a lifestyle, it has to be understood, but understanding own its own is not enough but rather the Word of God has to be believed and then lived. You can't understand the Word like this, "seek good and not evil that you may live", from Prophet Amos 5:4, since many people seeking evil are living, some long life to nearly a century.

What do you understand my dear? In my own understanding, if I have want to live I have to seek good physically and not evil. But, when I came to my belief, this Word of God is figuring out that seeking good and live, not evil means that the life of the person has got two sides that are the physical and spiritual banks. When you seek good, you are investing on both sides and alive as well, but when you do evil one bank is elapsed and that bank is the spiritual since evil is death for Apostle Paul had said that the only wages to sin is death. So my dear, seek good and not evil and you will live, amen. Then, coming to the real way to promise, I already alluded that the way is Jesus Christ, how? Allow the Word my brethren, to prove this for you. When God promised Abraham, the Father of all Nations that His descendants were going to live in a foreign land for more than 400years and then after that they went to their promised destiny.

The promise seemed to be bleak and unbearable before 400years were accomplished in Egypt, but after 400years, then it was able and bearable. On the 401st year, Israel thought that their time for Canaan heading journey had arrived but it wasn't the real time for the transition. The way to Canaan started that very year in the spiritual realm, thus the year God spoke to Moses through the burning bush. Moses argued with God, for he was knowing the people he was to be standing in the gap for and the people he was to confront in the whole process till vacation of Egypt. When the promise that God promised is being narrated to you sometimes, it is Greek to a Shona person. What! Someone might say that me a shaggy person who grew up in a lowest class of shaggy cabins in a squatter camp will make it to drive a trailblazer and own a mega house. Yes! My brother, the grace of the promise of God has located you. When the grace of God locates you, your very own mockers will be your workers.

Where is my climax now? The story here is climaxed on how to get the promise. Israel had been in captivity for 400years when they realised that God promised them a Canaan after 400years and they listened to Moses and Aaron. Remember, Israelites are the one who led Moses to flee from Egypt after Israelites black-labelled Moses as a murderer - a killer of Egyptian trying to deliver an Israelite. You can pray and fast for years but only a second in decision making can alter your prayers and fasting either into a great fortune or a great disaster. Israel accepted Moses as their deliverer, a back then murderer. My dear when God raised a Paul from Saul it is my desire for you to just accept it. Since, if you throw him out of your circle, you will be pushing Jesus Christ in Paul hence grieving the Holy Ghost. And as a result your promises from God will delay or even surpass you, so be careful.

I pray for you my sister, my brother, may your history or background lose you today in the name of Jesus Christ of Nazareth. May they both allow you to have an encounter with God as He will be calling you as a deliverer of your family. May God's grace locate you to rub off your history from Saul to Paul. And may Saul to Paul anointing fall upon you today in Jesus Christ's blessed and great name above all names. You were born to be a prophet to many nations, you were groomed to be priests and kings here on earth and you are destined for great exploits. Today through this script, I am moulding you to become one of those who will prophesy in these end times we are in. You shall be known all over the world, for you are of a peculiar generation. My dear brethren, you are not of this world, since the one who is in you is greater than the one who is in the world. You are born of spirit, full of spirit and you live in spirit.

Moses came into Egypt with only two signs backing up His words he heard from God. My dear, there is no Word of God without the backing of signs and wonders. There are preachers who are uncomfortable when they preach and someone manifests, they say shut up I want to preach, thus a borrowed deception from the devil. Why? It is just so, because what led that person to manifest is the Word of God you have just preached, deal with that issue while you are in the same spirit. Let the Word of God deliver that person from bondage, for Jesus Christ said that the Spirit of God is upon me to preach deliverance to the captives when He first entered the synagogues as He was from the wilderness. Then on another day, when He entered the synagogue to preach, a demon cried out saying that what have you to do with us Jesus Christ of Nazareth. He then instantly rebuked the evil spirit and He casted it out with His words.

My dear, the Word of God carries all the anointing and power you require to uproot anything planted in your life by the enemy. For St. John 1:1 says that in the beginning was the Word, the Word was with God and the Word was God. If you see yourself preaching the Word of God and no sign follows, my dear your preaching is not firmly rooted in the Word of God, thus that Word is not in its fullness. Since, the fullness of the Word of God brings in total deliverance to the hearer, as well as the preacher. On Romans 2:21, the Word of God says that you preach about not to steal or against stealing, yet you are still a great thief. Why can't you preach to yourself first before you preach to others. Moses went to Egypt to preach deliverance to Israelites after He had preached it to Himself and he was delivered from the spirit of murder and both him and the Israelites believed.

If you want people to trust and believe you here is a secret, live what you speak, live what you sing, live what you dream and live what you preach, amen. The way to your promise from God here look, Moses then went to Pharaoh and presented his case but Pharaoh denied the release of them for God had hardened Pharaoh's heart. When you realised and identified your promise, Satan will resist your access to your promise in form of giving you fleshy and worldly pleasures. Moses continued to believe and trust in God and later on Pharaoh accepted but look the Bible said God hardened Pharaoh's heart so that Pharaoh would refuse to let Israel go. Oh my Lord what a great strategy to shame the devil and his agents.

The Lord allowed Satan to enter pharaoh so as to find a cause for the destruction thus a prominent death of all Egyptians' first sons, calves, pigeons, lands, water and so forth. When God remembered you to be free from the bondage and get the fulfilment of God's promise, He will allow Satan to enter your enemy and hardens his enemy so as to find a cause for striking that enemy with leprosy hence paving a way for you to your destined promise. Egyptian leader lost many things but still hardened his heart. When God then stroked all first born Egyptians, Pharaoh realised that it wasn't no longer a joking area. When the frogs appeared, he (Pharaoh) said that they were going to cease for it was for that season only. Then as well God stopped the frogs plague latter. But, when he saw that all the first born had gone, he then realised that somewhere somehow he was the next one on the line to die, so he let them go. Oh my Lord!

When your enemy hardens his or her heart, don't worry keep on persevering, keep on knocking, keep on asking, keep on seeking, keep on doing good, and keep on glittering. My brother, my sister, never look back or downwards for that hardening of the enemies' hearts is just for God to find a justified reason for them to be punished. Allow your enemies to harden their hearts for God to then say to your enemies that because you have done these things now my wrath has located you the enemy of my child. My brethren, the time when God is allowing the hardening of the heart of the enemy is not the time to backslide but rather a time to dig deeper in the spiritual realm and go higher in the spirit. When Jesus was being denied by Peter, my Lord did not backslide but rather he cried in the spirit and he looked at Peter. And instantly, Peter get connected in spirit and he then started to cry for he remembered what Jesus Christ had been told him before.

Because of Peter's denial, I believe that strengthened my Lord better to stand before earthly rulers and judges. Here this, denial is not the dead end of you, but just a rejuvenation of your spirit. When future seems bleak my dear, God will then appear and a miracle will happen. When your promise is at the point of being like bleak, O my dear, don't worry, thus the beginning of your journey to your defined promise. The way to heaven is not wide enough for all people to fit in it but it's just for those that are willing and chosen. The way to paradise is narrow to suite the number going into it, for many were called but only the few were chosen. Likewise, the way to your promises is narrow, so as to allow only you the elected ones to get them. Israelites were many who knew the promise of Canaan from their birth, but they died still in bondage. Only those God had elected, Moses and Aaron, went to Pharaoh and presented their God's promise to Israel.

Many Israelites were called for the promise of Canaan, but only the promise was to be fulfilled to the chosen ones only. Thus why we see in the Word of God, Joshua and Caleb reaching Canaan without Moses and Aaron. If you want to see thus God's doing, God spoke to Moses and Aaron about the promise of Canaan, but it was then fulfilled in the eyes of Joshua and Caleb when Moses and Aaron were no longer there. Joshua and Caleb enjoyed honey and milk that was promised to Moses and Aaron. The promise might have been given to your forefathers but they haven't received them. My brother, my sister by the reason that you are their son by faith, take the Word of God and prevail over your enemies.

Prayer:

O Lord my God, father to the fatherless and husband to the widows, I pray thee O Lord may give us patience and strength to persevere for we know when things got tough for us, thus the ample given time for us to go higher in spirit and cause commotion in the kingdom of the devil. Thank you Lord for showing me that it takes only these four for me to have all your promises you promised us and declared to us – right mentality, positive attitude, hope and faith. My one and only heavenly Father, Jehovah Jireh, the only source and fountain of life, the provider of all material things, the healer of all diseases. I pray for myself, my family, may our history or background lose us today in the name of Jesus Christ of Nazareth. May the two both allow us to have an encounter with you God as you will be calling me as a deliverer of our family. May God's grace locate me to rub off my history from Saul to Paul. And may Saul to Paul anointing fall upon me today in Jesus Christ's blessed and great name above all names.

I was born to be a prophet to many nations, I was groomed to be a priest and a king here on earth and I am destined for great exploits. Today through this script, O Lord! I am being moulded to become one of those who will prophesy in these end times we are in. I shall be known all over the world, for I am one of a peculiar generation. My dear Father in heaven, I believe that I am not of this world, since the one who is in me is greater than the one who is in the world. I am born of spirit, full of spirit and I live in spirit, for I am of spirit. O Lord, many promises you have promised us but the truth is that all your promises are for those only who are aligned to your Word somewhere, somehow. O Lord, may you restore the zeal for you that has been in me. Help me that I may learn more about you and have a personal encounter with you in Jesus' name. Oh my dad, may you grant us our desires and may your name be glorified in Jesus Christ's name, I pray, amen.

Declarations:

I declare and I decree in the name of Jesus Christ that:

- I won't go out of my Egypt empty handed spiritually, mentally, economically and physically.
- My enemies will give me riches not to harm me but to prosper me, through the Lord's will.
- My life today will never be like my yesterday for I am uplifted in spirit and faith concerning God's promises.
- My mockers today will be my workers tomorrow since denial is not my destiny, it's just a rejuvenation of my journey to my destiny.
- No more delays in all the promises of God concerning my life.
- I am leaving a compromised lifestyle and transitioning into a separated lifestyle.
- No more conflicts in my belief because of my able Jesus Christ and I am highly elevated in my faith and knowledge in the Lord.
- All promises that have been delayed before are now in an acceleration mode to their manifestation in my life.
- All physical and spiritual promises God gave to Israel are mine and I am content to enjoy them.

- I am not hesitant to act upon each and every promise of God He promised to us through His Word.
- My future is brighter than my past and present, I will be announced when other will be ashamed.
- My tomorrow is glorious than my yesterday and my today, I will be fruitful in all my life endeavours.
- I will surely possess the gates of my enemies, it might not be today but definitely I will do it soon.
- I will witness all the promises of God in my life and enjoy all of them to the fullness.
- No more delays in all the promises of God concerning my life.
- I am leaving a compromised lifestyle and transitioning into a separated lifestyle.
- No more conflicts in my belief because of my able Jesus Christ and my life will never be the same again for the truth is setting me free and I shall not lack anything for all my needs are in God's promises, Amen.

Chapter 5: Promise Acquisition

Objectives:

- To know the proper time and season for God's promises to be acquired and have a realisation of the revelation behind promise acquisition.
- To have a glimpse of what it takes to acquire and to know who is to acquire promises God promised our forefathers.
- To understand the processes needed in promise acquisition as a process.

Here acquisition in my own opinion, I defined it as grabbing something gently or just calmly. Then, here in this context, promise acquisition, it is self-explanatory – define it with your own imagination. Promises are not just get, but there are stages to be followed. When the promise of honey and milk land came to Moses it was like a dream, but it was a reality. My dear time for your promise is coming you will be like dreaming. Remember, the Word of God says that when the captivity of Zion was by Babylon it ended like they were dreaming. A promise of God is a shocker to unbeliever, you will be like dreaming too. Coming back to Moses now, he started to give excuses as if him and his family were not in that bondage.

Many people today just because they were born in poverty they are seeing it as their proper lifestyle. When you reach them trying to preach a prosperity gospel to them they give you many excuses and reject it. My dear, I am here to tell you this, if you want to give space to your success, then kill your excuses. My dear, change your mentality my dear, your mentality determines your reality, your condition is not your conclusion. Brethren, change your language my brethren, begin to say what you imagine and see your life transitions. Moses said that he was not able to speak properly and not able to stand before pharaoh, my speech is not fluent.

My dear, when the promise of God comes into your life in the weakness part of you, never give any excuses. But what you have to do is to; speak it, believe it and receive it. What you confess is what you get, Apostle Paul said, that we are made unto salvation through the word of our mouths – thus confession through our mouths. I am wondering why Moses gave out those promises to God? Was it that he had forgotten his family, how badly they were being treated in Egypt.

When the grace of God comes into existence of your promise of God, my brethren, you start to give reasons to block it, but it won't change anything. Why? It is only because no one knows the thoughts and vision of God since God said out that His thoughts are not our thoughts. When the calling of God visits you, you start to give excuses; O Lord, I am not worthy it, for I am a prostitute; I am not worthy it, for I am a murderer. When apostle Paul saw the vision, he was still called Saul of Tarsus but he did not give any excuse for there was a sign that had appeared to him. So my dear don't worry when the promise acquisition time arrives, just understand, admit and then move on for it and with it.

When God remembers you my brethren, your mockers will be your workers, since God doesn't call the prepared nor the qualified but He qualifies those He has remembered. O my brother, my sister, those you met in your misery are the ones you will meet in your mysteries. My brethren, my message to you today is this, give a deaf ear to the devil when he puts a mountain before you. If you can't climb up the mountain to the other side, or tunnel through it, or even go either way of it on sides. Then know, it is time to speak and go forth through that mountain and grab your own promise.

Hannah saw the promise of fruitfulness and multiplication in the scrolls God promised to Adam n all his descendants. She saw that there was a possibility for her and she started to look for a time, a season and an opportunity to grab this promise. My dear when you see a possibility of a promise of God in your life, kill all excuses and start to be in look of a time, a season and an opportunity for you to receive that promise. For Hannah, when the time for her to grab her promise in the Lord, thus the time when Peninah started to block her and name tagging her to be a barren woman.

She gave a deaf ear to barrenness world her counterpart was saying she was in. Hannah then spoke forth a word to her God and then she begat the renowned Prophet of God – Samuel. Moses was name tagged a murderer, when the promise acquisition arrived and he fled away as if he was leaving the promise of God. You can run away from the call of God, but it will do nothing to the call of God but this will only delay you and not God. Moses from a murderer to a prophet, rather a God to Aaron, Paul from a murderer too to a great missionary, a greatest apostle rather. God can use you, even today the great Bok Haram soldiers can be turned into great preachers of the word of God in Nigeria.

Mary Magdalene is reported to be a great harlot, who then became a greatest evangelist and revelatory. She is the one that got the revelation of Jesus Christ death when she anointed and perfumed Jesus Christ. When Jesus Christ has gone into glory, she (Mary Magdalene) is seen going to the tomb with Salome and other Mary that I believe was Jesus Christ's earthly mother. Rahab too, a harlot of harlots, when God visited her she got the revelation of Israel spies hid. She did that and she served them and hid them in the inner room of her house. In doing so she saved herself and the rest of her family. She became a great and mighty deliverer to her family.

Don't let your current situation define your destiny, for your current condition is not your conclusion. Some circumstances we face in life are not according to God's plead but they are due to the plead of the devil. Job that day was stripped off from all his riches and wealth and was left with nothing due to the devil's plead in God's will. My dear your struggle is not your final story, joy is coming. The Word of God says that sorrow may come, but it will be just for a night, and joy will come in the morning. The situation you are facing today is not your set lifestyle but it is just temporary. Remember this always my dear, every time you feel like setting yourself backwards, God is looking at you to see if you are really sincere in him. A setback is a setup to your greatness.

Jairus's daughter was dead but when Jesus Christ looked at her, He said and I quote, "TALITHA'CUMI" meaning little girl rise up and walk. What am I trying to reveal here? My dear don't ever look at your current situation negatively but try to look on the positive part of your situation. Whether the positive part of your situation is ten percent and the rest ninety percent is negative, just look at that positive side. If there is no positive side of your current situation (meaning all around you is negative), then I urge you to find a polite and good picture to substitute it in your mind. On promise acquisition, never look at the number of people pursuing the same promise of God, just look at your life and concentrate on God and His promise. When God gave the promises He didn't mention the population to receive but He said those that believe will enjoy the fruits of God's promises.

Many people in life can study, can see, can even trace the promises of God but they then miss it on grabbing the promises – promise acquisition. Why? Many people we see acquisition of a promise as an instant act and not a process with a methodology. Here the methodology is believing, you can't instantly believe but you first have an understanding, then acquire knowledge and wisdom then believe. There were many widows in Israel but unto only one widow of Zarephath was Elijah sent by God. God had predestined that only that widow was to grab the that promise He gave to the widows. Acquisition of a promise of God is different from acquisition of a promise of a man, for God is not a man that He can lie or He should lie or He will lie. God is God.

Acquisition of a promise of God is determined by your attitude towards the promise of God and the faith you ought to have in Christ. Many people we that we have promises concerning our lives and day to day livings but our attitudes towards them are blocking us to get reach of them. How you perceive on the promises of God, gives you a glimpse of the outcome on them. Our duty today is not just look at the promises of God or to just know them but we have to take a step further in mentality transformation. Work on your mentality first before you work on your faith.

What is faith? Faith, now is the assurance of things hoped for but not seen with our physical eyes. Where do I get that hope? Hope is created after someone's mind imaginations. If you want to imagine correctly, positively transform your own mind-set. Oh my Lord, I like this, faith is taking a step u where there is no visible physical structure of a staircase but you are seeing the staircase in your own mind. Shamgar acquired the promise of possessing the gates of his enemies, after he acted upon the promise with a proper and positive attitude. Your positive attitude has to be integrated to a positive mind-set full of good imaginations leading to victory.

Shamgar's faith was then built up from the two – positive attitude and right mentality. And as a result, he grabbed that promise of God on possessing our enemies' gates. The story goes this way in a nutshell, Shamgar saw the enemies of Israel approaching Israel to devour Israel, then he looked among God's promises and he saw there was one in line with his enemies. There and there, he changed his mentality level from letting his enemies in and he reached to a mentality level of possessing his enemies' gates. He got that right mentality, took a positive attitude and then he worked on his faith basing on his hope. He slaughtered six hundred soldiers by an ox-goad and three hundred soldiers retreated.

My brethren as I close this chapter, allow me to tell you this message. No territory is small, no money is little, no one is small; but what led many to say that it is only the mentality. Many people are becoming billionaires today not because they are capable of being like that but just because they have the right mental attitude towards the subject. From today onwards my dear, change your mentality, have positive thoughts always and positive attitudes. Create good and best imaginations in your mind, for all things we see today they were once imaginations. My dear you were once an imagination in God's mind then later your parents' minds. Allow your imaginations to create a hope of your future. Using the good hope you have in Christ, then work on your faith, I see you grabbing your own promise of God concerning your life and the future with a bang. May God remember you as He did unto Mordecai. May God elevate you as He did unto Queen Esther. May God be with you as He did unto Daniel, amen.

Prayer:

O Lord, I pray in the name of Jesus Christ for all the words that I have read out, may I see that it was a new experience with you my Lord. Thank you Lord for showing me that it takes only these four for me to have all your promises you promised us and declared to us – right mentality, positive attitude, hope and faith. My one and only heavenly Father, Jehovah Jireh, the only source and fountain of life, the provider of all material things, the healer of all diseases. I pray thee today may you help us see with our spiritual eyes always that you are able. I pray for you myself, my family, may our history or background lose us today in the name of Jesus Christ of Nazareth. May they both allow you to have an encounter with God as He will be calling you as a deliverer of your family. May God's grace locates me to rub off my history from Saul to Paul.

And may Saul to Paul anointing fall upon me today in Jesus Christ's blessed and great name above all names. Today through this script, O Lord! I am being moulded to become one of those who will prophesy in these end times we are in. I shall be known all over the world, for I am one of a peculiar generation. My dear Father in heaven, I believe that I am not of this world, since the one who is in me is greater than the one who is in the world. I am born of spirit, full of spirit and I live in spirit, for I am of spirit.

O Lord, many promises you have promised us but the truth is that all your promises are for those only who are aligned to your Word somewhere, somehow. Lord, may you restore the zeal for you that has been in me that I may learn more about your and have a personal encounter with you in Jesus' name. May my mentality be changed from today onwards, may I only see the positive and have only positive imaginations and hope of my future in the name of Jesus Christ, Amen.

Declarations:

I declare and I decree in the name of Jesus Christ that;

- My mentality has shifted to a higher positive realm, and I am no longer looking for minor things but I am after better things in the Lord.
- The Lord has granted me all promises He promised to me and my forefathers.
- My attitude, hope and faith have changed, for the Lord has inspired me to be a better believer.
- My faith is about to do exploits in my life and I am about to see good, better and best results from today onwards.
- All God's promises to Abraham are mine and I am going to live an Abrahamic lifestyle.

- Many will come to congratulates me on this great boom, for these promises of God are a great boom.
- No more delays in all the promises of God concerning my life.
- I am leaving a compromised lifestyle and transitioning into a separated lifestyle.
- No more conflicts in my belief because of my able Jesus Christ and I am highly elevated in my faith and knowledge in the Lord.
- All promises that have been delayed before are now in an acceleration mode to their manifestation in my life.
- All physical and spiritual promises God gave to Israel are mine and I am content to enjoy them.
- I am not hesitant to act upon each and every promise of God He promised to us through His Word.
- My future is brighter than my past and present, I will be announced when other will be ashamed.
- My tomorrow is glorious than my yesterday and my today, I will be fruitful in all my life endeavours.
- I will surely possess the gates of my enemies, it might not be today but definitely I will do it soon.
- I will witness all the promises of God in my life and enjoy all of them to the fullness.

- No more delays in all the promises of God concerning my life.
- I am leaving a compromised lifestyle and transitioning into a separated lifestyle.
- My life will never be the same again for the truth is setting me free and I shall not lack anything for all my needs are in God's promises, Amen.

Chapter 6: *Promise* Conduction

Objectives:

- To thrive for making perfection our priority of living in this world.
- To capture a revelatory encounter and experience in the promises of God.
- To know terms and conditions for the promise to last long for your benefit.
- To understand the principles of living in the promises of God.

Conduction means the way things has to be done. In this context, conduction is implying to be that which a believer is to do after acquiring the promise of God. This is how the believer who had acquired God's promise is going to live in the promise and with that promise. In other words, these are terms and conditions applied in conduction. For a promise to be a promise, there has to be conditions before and after promise acquisition. In conduction, we are talking of fulfilling what you have told God, thus oaths you have given to God – vows you have vowed to God.

Look at what happened to Hannah, what led Hannah to acquire a promise of God concerning fruitfulness? She begat Samuel – the

Prophet as a promise from God as a result of her vows. Due to the fact that she had vowed to God corning the baby, God gave the baby to her. The vow wasn't easy to implement but out of disgrace by Peninah she got courage. She gave an oath that the baby was going be the Lord's not hers. She adds on to say that the son was to be according to God's will not her will. Time for the acquisition of the promise came and she grabbed all corners of fruitfulness and multiplication.

Then in conducting the acquired promise of God, she nurtured Samuel well in a good manner. When Samuel had well grown, she then fulfilled her promise as well to God. My dear, a promise of God is accompanied by your promise as well to Him. Promises of God to His people are always in line with the promises of people to God as well. Hannah went with Samuel to the priest – Eli and surrendered the boy to God as she had vowed. Coming closer to you, my dear brethren whatsoever you have vowed before the manifestation of the Lord do accordingly for God is not a man that He should lie. Whatever He vowed to you; He fulfilled, He is fulfilling and He will fulfil it.

My dear brethren, if you want God to bless you highly in the conduction highway of the promise, just fulfil your vows and declarations to God. Many at times we fail in life not because we are failures but because we are liars to God. We vow to God and forget our vows but the fact is God is not a man hence His ways and thoughts are neither similar to ours. When in the conduction phase, the permit or route of authority is faith. The word of God said that faith comes by hearing, and hearing by the Word of God. What is faith then? Faith now is the assurance of things hoped for but not yet seen or received.

When the Israelites received the promise of Canaan, God gave an order for them to borrow from Egyptians all jewelleries they desire by faith. Israelites came out of Egypt full handed and richly in debts. God did this to find a cause for pharaoh to follow after them to be drowned as it was prophesised. Pharaoh ordered a follow up of Israel. I don't believe he was pursuing not people only. The golden jewelleries they have borrowed from Egyptians that which we later saw them building up a golden calf of gold was in Pharaoh. I do not know how big the size of the calf was, but what I know and I am certain of is that it was not only a gram of gold that made up the calf. I approximately predict that they were kilograms of gold that built up the body of the calf.

Viewing from another angle, when the Israelites saw the army of pharaoh approaching them, they said that Moses we are about to perish here. They knew what was the matter about, it was not about them leaving Egypt. How come Pharaoh who once accepted them to leave then latter on said pursue them? I believe the issue is that when he accepted their departure he didn't knew gold was to varnish from their people in jewellery and so forth. People came to report that the Israelites had dubbed them and all jewellery had gone. Pharaoh noticed that he was in danger of his people rebelling against him, so he sent the army. Only getting out of Egypt was not a big crime but the corruption they had done was a threat to Egypt's economy.

Israelites when they saw the army approaching, they were frightened not because they have left Egypt but they were not able to pay back all the jewellery they had borrowed. It was a threat to their lives thus why you hear them crying saying that it was better for them to die in Egypt than to die in the forest near wilderness. My dear, if it of God and from God none of the critics will wipe you away. In this context, due to the token and vindicated Word of God they had believed in they conquered. Moses their Prophet under inspiration was heard shouting to them that those Egyptians they were seeing pursuing them, after that day they will see them no more. My dear, in your life you might have many Egyptians pursuing you physically and spiritually, don't worry.

I stand in the gap today under the same inspiration Moses got and declare that those Egyptians you are seeing today you will see them no more. Life is not all about seeing things happening but also believing things are happening is an attribute of life. Moses just spoke out those words before even talking or seeing God that day. My dear at times, it is not about seeing or hearing God that will render you your victory. Having a right mental attitude, full of good zeal and a mouth full of positive words is enough. What you speak of gives you faith and hope. If faith comes by hearing this means it can come by speaking as well, amen. Whatsoever you want to see or you desire to be, the way to it is simple you have to keep on saying it.

God will surely back you up, if your faith, belief and hope are centred on him in accompany with a right mental attitude. Some say that your attitude determines your altitude. Moses spoke and it came to pass as the Egyptians got drowned in the Red Sea. Sometimes poverty is pursuing you, my dear have the right mental attitude against it, then speak a positive word of faith, put your trust in the Lord and finally conquer poverty. If you are not yet there, then you have to create a state of mind in which you will be seeing yourself as the C.E.O of a great group of companies. Let me tell you this, I became a C.E.O of my company when I was grade one. This came in as a result of my grade one class teacher who used to say that Talent and company keep quiet or else I will ask you to go out to talk.

Going back to my chapter context, allow me to say this, all the promises of God are there to really define the real stature of a real man like what Peter mentioned in the Word of God (2 Peter 5:8). For instance, Jeremiah 29:11 states that the Lord knows the plans He have for you, plans not to harm you, but plans for the good future and a great hope with an expected end. When the promise of God is now being conducted in one's life, thus the time when God will really take your mind into His own mind and show you the reason why He created you. In conduction God will review you who you are and how great you are. What God require of us most is not money, clothes, food, drink, parties, refreshment or resorts.

So what is it that He demands? He only demands a holy and pure life. God requires you to satisfy His will through the life you live. He cries and desires you live a holy life, not for his benefit but for your own beneficial. If you want to live a long life, then consider your ways very well. Some of sicknesses and diseases are caused by not following God's principles. All that is contrary to the Word of God is abuse to the body, for the body God gave you is a residential place for the Holy Spirit. If you have got a desire to see the promises of God manifesting in your life, the journey is short. You have to consider your ways, repent and confess your sins. Let confession, be your first priority, for through mouth confession, salvation is made unto them.

Prayer:

O Lord God of Abraham, Isaac and Jacob, I pray today with all my faith based on my hearings from the Word of God. My heavenly father I am your son(daughter) hear my cry for a father always pay attention to the call through a cry of His child. May your mercies rain upon my life today that I may testify that God is with me. Help me O Lord to change my mind attitude, give me O Lord a right mental attitude. I pray for you my sister, my brother, may your history or background lose you today in the name of Jesus Christ of Nazareth. May the two both allow you to have an encounter with God as He will be calling you as a deliverer of your family. May God's grace locate me to rub off my history from Saul to Paul. And may Saul to Paul anointing fall upon you today in Jesus Christ's blessed and great name above all names. I was born to be a prophet to many nations, I was groomed to be a priest and king here on earth and you are destined for great exploits.

Today through this script, O Lord! I am being moulded to become one of those who will prophesy in these end times we are in. I shall be known all over the world, for I am one of a peculiar generation. My dear Father in heaven, I believe that I am not of this world, since the one who is in me is greater than the one who is in the world. I am born of spirit, full of spirit and I live in spirit, for I am of spirit. O Lord, many promises you have promised us but the truth is that all your promises are for those only who are aligned to your Word somewhere, somehow. Lord, may you restore the zeal for you that has been in me that I may learn more about your and have a personal encounter with you in Jesus' name. May my mentality be changed from today onwards, may I only see the positive and have only positive imaginations and hope of my future in the name of Jesus Christ. Recreate in me a new heart, O Lord, I pray thee. Shift my eyes away from the things that are contrary to the process of getting your promises in the name of Jesus Christ of Nazareth. Give me a zeal for you O Lord that I may do your will in all my life endeavours, Amen.

Declarations:

- All physical and spiritual promises God gave to Israel are mine and I am content to enjoy them.
- I am not hesitant to act upon each and every promise of God He promised to us through His Word.
- My future is brighter than my past and present, I will be announced when other will be ashamed.

- My tomorrow is glorious than my yesterday and my today, I will be fruitful in all my life endeavours.
- I will surely possess the gates of my enemies, it might not be today but definitely I will do it soon.
- I will witness all the promises of God in my life and enjoy all of them to the fullness.
- No more delays in all the promises of God concerning my life.
- I am leaving a compromised lifestyle and transitioning into a separated lifestyle.
- No more conflicts in my belief because of my able Jesus Christ and I am highly elevated in my faith and knowledge in the Lord.
- All promises that have been delayed before are now in an acceleration mode to their manifestation in my life.
- My life will never be the same again for the truth is setting me free and I shall not lack anything for all my needs are in God's promises.
- I am now inspired to aspire to be a blessing to the whole world and I am living to bless people, world at large and not to be blessed by the world.
- I got the revelation that the all promises of God are mine and I am highly elevated in Christ and for Christ.

- No more limitations in the name of Jesus Christ and I am destined for greater exploits to be explored.
- Now am highly enlightened to be at a point of knowing what to do to get my promise manifestation. No more delays in all the promises of God concerning my life.
- I am leaving a compromised lifestyle and transitioning into a separated lifestyle.
- My mentality has shifted to a higher positive realm, and I am no longer looking for minor things but I am after better things in the Lord.
- The Lord has granted me all promises He promised to me and my forefathers.
- My attitude, hope and faith have changed, for the Lord has inspired me to be a better believer.
- My faith is about to do exploits in my life and I am about to see good, better and best results from today onwards.
- All God's promises to Abraham are mine and I am going to live an Abrahamic lifestyle.
- Many will come to congratulates me on this great boom, for these promises of God are a great boom.
- I won't go out of my Egypt empty handed spiritually, mentally, economically and physically.

- My enemies will give me riches not to harm me but to prosper me, through the Lord's will.
- My life today will never be like my yesterday for I am uplifted in spirit and faith concerning God's promises.
- My mockers today will be my workers tomorrow since denial is not my destiny, it's just a rejuvenation of my journey to my destiny, Amen

Lord's Prayer

Our Father which art in heaven,
Hallowed be Thy name. Thy Kingdom come,
Thy will be done in earth, as it is in heaven.

Give us this day our daily bread.

And forgive our debts, as we forgive our debtors.
And lead us not into temptations,
But deliver us from evil:

For thine is the Kingdom, and the power,
And the glory for ever, Amen.
(Matthew 6:9 – 13)

Author

The author of this book went to a Catholic mission school in Masvingo and there he learnt a lot. In between the years 2010 and 2015, he won several academic certificates. Apart from academic, in 2011 he proudly attained overall best male ZJC smartness prize. In 2014, he was award a church liturgy certificate. As a result, this gave him a challenge even to seek more and more on how to impact the society around him. He then started to write some short inspirational messages on all his social media platform i.e. facebook, whatsapp, instagram, twitter.

Due to the feedback, and criticism he got from the social platforms, he came up with the only answer as a solution to the cry of his followers, that was to be definitely a writer. This book titled, **"Reinforcement onto God's Promises"** is his first and foremost book he wrote and published. On the other angle, he is understanding a Bachelor of Technology(Hons.) degree in Electronic Engineering. He is a writer by passion and life & business coach by calling. And this vibrant leader is none other than Talent Blessing Mukaro Matuhwa.

www.ingramcontent.com/pod-product-compliance
Ingram Content Group UK Ltd.
Pitfield, Milton Keynes, MK11 3LW, UK
UKHW041919190726
13854UKWH00003B/1334

9 780359 142804